basketball's
new wave

Kevin
Garnett

Shake Up the Game

BY
MARK STEWART

THE MILLBROOK PRESS
BROOKFIELD, CONNECTICUT

M

THE MILLBROOK PRESS

Produced by
BITTERSWEET PUBLISHING
John Sammis, President
and
TEAM STEWART, INC.
RESEARCHED AND EDITED BY MIKE KENNEDY

Series Design and Electronic Page Makeup by
JAFFE ENTERPRISES
Ron Jaffe

All photos courtesy AP/ Wide World Photos, Inc., except the following:
AllSport — Cover
Columbia, SC, Chamber of Commerce — Page 7
Greenville News © 1993 — Page 10
The following images are from the collection of Team Stewart:
ROOX Corp. © 1995 — Page 15
Time Inc./Sports Illustrated © 1995 — Page 18
ESPN/ESPN the Magazine © 1999 — Page 35

Printed in the United States of America

Published by
The Millbrook Press, Inc.
2 Old New Milford Road
Brookfield, Connecticut   06804

www.millbrookpress.com

Library of Congress Cataloging-in-Publication Data

Stewart, Mark.
    Kevin Garnett : shake up the game / by Mark Stewart.
        p. cm. — (Basketball's new wave)
    Includes index.
    Summary: A biography of the Minnesota Timberwolves star forward, Kevin Garnett.
    ISBN 0-7613-2615-4
    1. Garnett, Kevin, 1976—Juvenile literature. 2. Basketball players—United States—
Biography—Juvenile literature. [1. Garnett, Kevin, 1976- 2. Basketball players. 3.
African Americans—Biography.] I. Title: Shake up the game. II. Title. III. Series.

GV884.G37 S84 2002
796.323'092—dc21
[B]   2001044420

1 3 5 7 9 10 8 6 4 2

Contents

The Kid Is All Right

chapter 1

*"I know what it is
like to have nothing."*

— KEVIN GARNETT

Kevin Garnett is known around the NBA as Da Kid. That seems strange to most fans. When they look at Kevin, they see a tower of power, a mountain of muscle—a man with a deep voice, proud posture, and a long list of career accomplishments. He is a regular at the NBA All-Star Game, he has earned All-NBA honors, and he even won a gold medal as a member of the United States Olympic team. It is easy to forget that he achieved all of these things before he blew out the candles on his 25th birthday cake.

Kevin prefers to go by his initials. But KG doesn't mind his nickname. In fact, he gets a kick out of it. When the pressure is on and everyone in the arena is expecting him to dominate a game, it is Da Kid inside him that comes out. And in no time, everyone gets caught up in his enthusiasm. "I go crazy trying to energize people," Kevin

Kevin Garnett may be a veteran, but when he wins he feels like a kid again.

Ever since he was a kid, Kevin's intensity and energy have rubbed off on his teammates.

smiles. "I'm a battery. If you're down, you can plug into me and get charged up. I've been a leader practically my whole life. I don't know what it *is* to follow."

Indeed, it is Kevin's ability to inspire those around him that makes it so hard to remember he is still a "baby" by basketball standards. Yet he has come a long, long way since 1995, when he made headlines as the first teenager in 20 years to jump directly from high school to the NBA.

Kevin knows where his boundless energy and upbeat attitude come from: his mom. In 1976, Shirley Garnett brought Kevin into the world as a single mother. She raised Kevin and his sisters, Sonya and Ashley, with little help from family and friends. Shirley did not always have the time to spend with her children, but she made the time anyway. Kevin, the middle kid, learned a lot. "In a woman's house, she taught me respect—that to get respect, you must give it," he says. "I learned respect by watching her work her tail off to provide for us."

The Garnetts lived in Columbia, South Carolina, a city of around 50,000 residents. People called their neighborhood Nickeltown. The houses were old and creaky, and the families mostly African American. Kevin liked Nickeltown. He did not like being poor, however. "You look at things much differently when you wash out your own socks at night and then wear them the next day," Kevin says. "I'll never forget what those days were like, or forget where I came from."

Shirley Garnett often pulled double-shifts at a nearby factory, and also worked as a hair stylist. From time to time she received money from Kevin's father, O'Lewis

McCullough. After Kevin was born his father married another woman and started a family of his own. Shirley appreciated his support, but did not encourage contact between Kevin and the McCullough clan. Kevin finally figured out he had a lot of relatives in Nickeltown when he met one of his cousins, Shammond Williams, in elementary school. Shammond filled Kevin in on the family picture. Soon he was spending time with his grandparents, Odell and Mary McCullough, who owned a home a few blocks away.

Kevin's father was not much of an influence in his life. But he did "give" Kevin something important: a special talent for basketball. In the early 1970s, O'Lewis McCullough was known around Columbia as Bye-Bye

Did You Know?

In high school, Kevin's father wore number 45 and was a great open-court player. When he got the ball on the fast break, everyone would say "bye-bye 45!" as he streaked to the basket.

45. He was the star of the Beck High School basketball team. He had the size of a forward, the skills of a guard, and the power moves of a center. Unfortunately, when the

Magic Johnson, who inspired Kevin to become history's first "seven-foot guard"

college scouts came to see McCullough, they came away fearing he would not be quick enough to play guard or tall enough to be a good college rebounder. When no scholarships came his way, he enlisted in the Army and continued to play in amateur leagues. He was still a local legend when Shirley met him.

Shirley remarried when Kevin was seven, but his stepfather, Ernest Irby, did not like basketball. So when Kevin was feeling low, basketball became a father and a friend to him. Whenever he was bored or angry or upset, he would go down to the playground. Sometimes, when he could not sleep, he would grab a ball, sneak out of his window, and head down the street. "When I didn't have a friend, when I was lonely, I always knew I could grab that orange pill and go hoop," he remembers. "If things weren't going right, I could make a basket and feel better."

Kevin played basketball for hours on end. He tried to copy Magic Johnson of the Lakers, a 6-foot 9-inch (206-centimeter) guard who electrified crowds with his twisting drives and dazzling no-look passes. Kevin was by far the tallest kid in his class, and he often dreamed of following in Magic's footsteps. "I always wanted to be the first seven-foot point guard," he laughs.

Growing Up Fast

chapter 1

"I'd like people to think of me
as a young adult instead of a kid."
— KEVIN GARNETT

When Kevin was twelve, he discovered a group of boys who shared his passion for basketball. The Garnetts had just moved from Nickeltown to Mauldin, a small town just a few miles away. There, on Basswood Drive, he found a pickup game whenever he wanted. Most of the kids were older and stronger than Kevin. When his mother saw the size of these kids, she told him to "think big"—to work and improve and find ways to be better. This advice has echoed in his head ever since. "If you think small and accomplish it," maintains Kevin, "what does it mean? Who cares? To me the sky's the limit, and I'm going to try and get there."

Kevin improved rapidly in those pickup games. Within a couple of years he stood out from those boys, both in size and skill. He did not understand much about strategy or team play, however. This showed when he went out for the Mauldin High School varsity as a freshman in 1991. Kevin seemed confused at times, and did not anticipate well. But Coach James Fisher liked his raw talent and decided to keep him on the team. Kevin blossomed under Fisher in his freshman season and averaged 12.5 points, 14 rebounds, and 7 blocks per game.

Kevin towers above an opponent in a game for Mauldin High.

The following summer, Kevin joined a local team that belonged to the Amateur Athletic Union (AAU), a national organization that oversees sports leagues for teenagers. The coach, Darren Gazaway, loved Kevin. He reported early for games and workouts, and went right to the playground afterward. Whatever had worked that day, Kevin would practice until it was perfect. Whatever had *not* worked, he would practice until it *did* work.

Another thing Coach Gazaway liked was that, whenever Kevin got the ball, his first instinct was to look for the teammate with the best chance to score. When the other players realized this, they worked extra-hard to get open. Kevin was making his teammates better—the first sign of a future superstar. Of course, he enjoyed scoring as much as anyone. By this time Kevin could dunk the ball, and it made him feel great to hear the crowd ooh and aah. Still, he got just as much pleasure from rejecting an opponent's shot or "threading the needle" with a perfect outlet pass.

When the Mauldin High team began practicing in the fall of 1992, Coach Fisher barely recognized Kevin. Not only had he grown several inches over the summer, he was also an astonishingly talented player and a leader his teammates naturally followed. Kevin dominated as a rebounder and defender. He was a terrific ball handler and playmaker. He could shake a defender loose with a couple of quick moves, and had the body control to slice to the basket or pull up for a quick jumper. When the team needed inside scoring, Kevin simply backed in toward the lane and called for the ball. He had a complete arsenal of power moves, plus a deadly turn-around shot. In short, he was unguardable.

What Coach Fisher liked most about Kevin was that he was not "uncoachable." Often when a young player discovers his skills, he hogs the ball and stops listening to advice. Kevin was just the opposite. He strained to soak up every word during practices and timeouts. If Fisher suggested Kevin try something new, or asked him to do something differently, he did not ask why. He just did it.

What Kevin's teachers and fellow students liked most about him was that he did not act like a star. He participated enthusiastically in class and treated everyone with respect and kindness. He had little choice, of course. Had his mother heard he was being a jerk, Kevin would have been grounded for life!

Malik and Me

In the early 1990s, Malik Sealy was busy making a name for himself as the star of the St. John's University basketball team. Little did he know that a teenager more than 500 miles (805 kilometers) away was making him his role model. "I was trying to find someone who was 'another me,'" Kevin says. "Not the best player, but someone who played like me. Malik Sealy was at St. John's at the time, and I just related to him. He was quick, dark-skinned, had long arms, and he mad-dunked."

Kevin says his amazing "metamorphosis" during the summer of 1992 came as a result of studying Sealy's game. When he returned to Mauldin, he requested his hero's number 21—a number he still wears today.

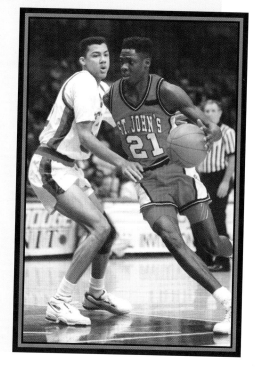

Wrong Place, Wrong Time

chapter

*"My idea is, 'I shine, you shine—
if I'm doing well and you're
with me, you do well.'"*

— KEVIN GARNETT

Kevin continued to sharpen his game during his junior year. He averaged 27 points and 17 rebounds, and led the Mauldin Mavericks to the state championship. After the season, Kevin was named South Carolina's Mr. Basketball—an honor that had been reserved exclusively for seniors until Kevin came along. Everything was perfect in Kevin's world.

Until an afternoon in May, when a fight broke out at Mauldin High between a white student and several black students. Moments after it started, punches were being thrown everywhere, as dozens of kids got involved. There was a lot of pushing and shoving and grappling, and Kevin found himself in the middle of it all, watching the melee from 6 feet 10 inches (208 cm) off the ground.

Being touted as a future NBA star almost ended Kevin's career before it started.

The police were summoned. They broke up the fight and decided to arrest everyone they could lay their hands on. Back at the police station, detectives attempted to sort out who did what to whom. When they realized that the famous Kevin Garnett was in custody, they saw a chance to get a little publicity. Kevin was charged with the absurd crime of "second-degree lynching."

When Kevin's friends heard about the charges, they laughed out loud. If there was one kid in town who could not have been involved in such madness it was Kevin. Besides, South Carolina's lynching laws were created decades earlier to protect blacks against white mobs. Many were surprised that they were still on the books, certain they were never meant to be applied to a situation like this.

Still, there was nothing funny about what happened next. Despite the fact that Kevin proclaimed his innocence—and that there was no solid evidence against him—the charges were not dropped. Kevin's name was splashed across the headlines of every newspaper in the South. His story was reported on television and radio, too. No matter what Kevin did or said, people now thought of him as a brutal giant who went around lynching people. Eventually, the matter was settled and the charges were dropped. But it was too late for Kevin. People treated him differently after that. They whispered when he walked by, and turned away when he fixed his gaze upon them.

Many thought Kevin was guilty, but that he had used his celebrity to get out of trouble. Some say the authorities were guilty of using Kevin's fame to draw attention to themselves. The truth may never be known. All Shirley Garnett knew was that her son

was in pain. Many of Kevin's friends had pulled away, and even Coach Fisher treated him as if he had done something bad. Kevin's mother felt it would be cruel to keep such a friendly young man in such an unfriendly place. She decided to take Kevin out of Mauldin and let him finish high school somewhere else.

As he had always done in times of trouble, Kevin lost himself in his basketball. His AAU team dominated opponents all summer and won the prestigious Kentucky Hoopfest tournament. Later in the summer, he accepted an invitation to attend a special camp run by Nike for the nation's top high-school players. While there, Kevin struck up a friendship with Ronnie Fields. Fields attended the Farragut Academy in Chicago, which had an excellent basketball team. He knew that Kevin was looking to get out of South Carolina and suggested he apply to the school. One thing led to another, and soon his mother was talking to Farragut officials. Kevin was accepted and, a few weeks later, he and his

How many athlete's have a high-school rookie card? This is Kevin's, from 1995.

mother and younger sister, Ashley, rented an apartment in Chicago.

Kevin was happy at Farragut, but surprised and disappointed when his past caught up to him that fall. Rumors began circulating that the real reason he left Mauldin was that he had flunked out. That made Kevin look bad, and made his new school look bad, too. Although basketball is a big deal at Farragut, it is proud of its academic reputation. Kevin just kept saying he wanted a fresh start, and that he looked forward to a competitive season. Eventually, the reporters and camera crews went away.

Of course, they came back a few months later, when Kevin put his basketball skills on display. Playing center for the Admirals, he astounded everyone who saw him. The quality of play in and around Chicago is much better than anything Kevin faced in South Carolina, yet he was even better against the better players. Coach William Nelson had expected a "project" when he was told Kevin was coming to Farragut in the fall of 1994. He quickly realized that his project would be to find ways he could improve Kevin's game!

As Farragut's season progressed, there were more writers and photographers and more college recruiters in

Did You Know?

At the 1994 Beach Ball Classic in Myrtle Beach, South Carolina, Kevin was asked for his autograph for the first time.

the stands at each game. There were even a few NBA scouts "stopping in" to see what all the commotion was about. At the Coca-Cola/KMOX Shootout in December, representatives from a dozen pro teams were in the stands to watch Farragut play its first important game, against the Vashon Wolverines.

"When I first saw him, he had the best athletic skills for his size of anyone I had ever seen at that stage."

ELGIN BAYLOR

The Admirals played poorly in the first half, with Kevin scoring just four points and committing several turnovers. Vashon built a 15-point lead in the third quarter, when Kevin finally woke up. He remembered that he was at his best when he was a "puzzle piece," not the whole picture. Kevin made some big plays on defense, hit a couple of shots and threw some good passes, and Farragut started to roll. With a furious rally, the Admirals squeezed out a 58–55 victory.

The scouts were impressed. Most young stars would have attempted to take over a game like this and to try to do more than they could. Kevin had actually toned down his game and let his teammates play a big role in the comeback. At eighteen, he already understood there is more than one way to dominate a game. "One thing that showed was his com-

Did You Know?

Kevin was named 1995 High School Player of the Year by USA TODAY.

petitiveness," said one talent evaluator afterward. "He wants to win as badly as anybody on the floor, and you want to see that in a superstar."

Decisions, Decisions

chapter 4

*"He is not ready for the
NBA. He'd get eaten alive."*
— NBA DRAFT EXPERT MARTY BLAKE

Kevin had impressed the pro scouts and he knew it. He had long dreamed of going straight from high school to the NBA, but suspected that his mother would frown on skipping college. So whenever anyone asked, he would say things like: "College is next. It's not about basketball. You can't just skip to a whole different level. It is a different level of maturity."

Although he was enjoying all the attention, Kevin knew he would have to make a decision soon. Several top schools were offering scholarships, including the universities of Michigan, Illinois, and Kentucky. They considered him a player who might deliver a national championship. They liked his skills, his attitude, and his grades. Kevin was doing well at Farragut, with a B+ average. The NBA, however, was still very tempting.

Making Kevin's decision a bit trickier was that he knew something the recruiters did not: He was terrible at taking tests. And in order to play Division I sports in college, you need to score well on the college entrance exams. Kevin enrolled in a class to

Kevin's decision to enter the NBA Draft made him a SPORTS ILLUSTRATED cover story.

improve his test-taking skills, but he still froze up during practice exams. If that happened on the real test, he would not be allowed to play in college for a year. That would be the most miserable thing he could imagine.

As decision day neared, Kevin began to think more seriously about the NBA, and the NBA began to think more seriously about him. No one doubted that Kevin had the skills to succeed, but did he have the body? He was a lean and sinewy 6 feet, 11 inches (211 cm), and weighed only 220 pounds (100 kilograms). Players that tall in the NBA usually have an additional 30 to 50 pounds (14 to 23 kg) of muscle on their bones. Kevin would look like a sapling among oak trees!

With Kevin improving every game, Farragut went on to win the state championship. In March, he took the college entrance exam and, as expected, scored below the cutoff. The NBA was looking better and better.

That April, Kevin was invited to St. Louis for the 18th annual McDonald's All-American High School Game. Among the teenagers at the tournament were future stars Vince Carter, Paul Pierce, Ron Mercer, and Shareef Abdur-Rahim. Also on hand was Stephon Marbury, a meteoric point guard from the Coney Island section of Brooklyn. Kevin and Stephon had become phone friends the previous summer. He had called Kevin after hearing about his legal troubles, and since then the two ran up enormous telephone bills chatting for hours about video games, girls, colleges, and basketball.

The two friends suited up for different sides in the game, with Kevin playing for the West team and Marbury for the East. Kevin was magnificent in a 126–115 victory, with 18 points and 11 rebounds—a performance that earned him the John Wooden Trophy as player of the game. Poor Jelani McCoy, an excellent player in his own right, had to stand in Kevin's shadow all day.

In the weeks that followed, there was more debate about whether Kevin was ready for the NBA. By this time it was clear that he would be selected among the first dozen picks. Maryland's Joe Smith was expected to go first, but after that it was anyone's guess. Among the premier players were Jerry Stackhouse, Antonio McDyess, Rasheed Wallace, and Damon Stoudamire. Scouts rated Kevin just a notch below this group.

Needless to say, Kevin was flattered to be rated so high. But he was also scared that he might be getting in over his head. In 1976 another talented high schooler named Bill Willoughby jumped from a small private school in New Jersey directly to the NBA and he was overwhelmed. At a time when Willoughby should have been enjoying his prime years, he was already out of the league. On the other hand, Kevin saw the suc-

cess of Moses Malone, who joined the American Basketball Association straight from high school in 1974. Malone was tall and skinny like Kevin. He was banged around for a couple of years, but eventually developed into an MVP.

Kevin was days away from having to decide between college and the pros, and he still was not sure. He took the SAT exam—his last chance to qualify for college acceptance. He also asked Eric Fleisher, a well-known Chicago sports agent, to evaluate his chances. Fleisher took him to a local gym and watched him work out. Kevin was nervous and looked awkward at times. Fleisher was

Moses Malone (24) skipped college to join the pros and became a Hall of Famer.

"This was my first draft. Our owner was also new. How do you tell him that the first thing he's going to do is sign this high school kid? I figured if it went bad, we'd just say, 'Hey, it was our first draft. We didn't know what we were doing.'"

KEVIN MCHALE

not impressed. Kevin halted his workout and asked if he could join the pickup game at the other end of the gym. Fleisher agreed, and watched as Kevin took control of the game.

Convinced that Kevin could hold his own in the NBA, Fleisher told him he should go pro if that is what his heart said. Kevin decided to enter the draft and held a press conference to announce his choice. Most sportswriters thought he was crazy. They believed Kevin lacked the maturity, work habits, street smarts, and physical size to survive. Some changed their minds after Kevin blew away other potential first-round picks during special predraft scrimmages, but right up until draft day there were more skeptics than believers.

Kevin's biggest believer was Kevin McHale, the new Vice President of Operations for the Minnesota Timberwolves. McHale, who also stood a shade under 7 feet (213 cm) tall, had played his entire NBA career at 220 pounds (100 kg), and was one of the greatest all-around forwards. Initially, he had dismissed the possibility of drafting Kevin, but had been impressed after attending one of the special scrimmages. In six seasons, the Timberwolves had never won more than 29 games. They had a new owner, who promised fans a "new era." Was it crazy to start that new era by drafting a high-school player?

After a lot of soul-searching, McHale believed Kevin was exactly what the team needed. He selected Kevin with the fifth pick in the draft. That night, Coach Nelson called Kevin to congratulate him. He also informed him that he had just received his scores from the SAT.

"You passed," he said.

"Well," sighed Kevin, "it's too late now."

Teen Wolf

chapter 5

> *"I don't care how good you are.*
> *I care how good you will be."*
> — KEVIN MCHALE

After the excitement of the draft had died down a bit, Kevin and his agent sat down with the Timberwolves and started mapping out a plan. The first order of business was to make Kevin a millionaire—he agreed to a three-year contract worth more than $5 million. The second order of business was to figure out how to keep Minnesota's youngest millionaire focused and out of trouble.

Everyone agreed that Kevin should have friends and family nearby. So he rented a two-bedroom apartment in Minneapolis and invited a couple of buddies from South Carolina to live with him. Then they bought three dogs. Kevin also

> *"Even though I'm not going to college right away, it is still important to me. I plan to take some classes when I can."*
> **KEVIN GARNETT**

Kevin throws one down during his rookie season.

moved his mother to Minnesota, and leased an apartment for her, too. He even found a couple of substitute fathers in Jimmy Jam and Terry Lewis—a pair of Grammy-winning record producers who could give a young man advice on avoiding the pitfalls of fame. They told Kevin to call them any time, and he did. To this day they are still like family.

Kevin got to know his teammates, coaches, trainers, and the team's office staff over the summer. When training camp opened in October, he was feeling right at home. Still, he was surprised by the intensity of NBA practices. "I never thought two-a-days could be so rough," he says. "When you think you're about to get a break, you don't get one. I just had to stop thinking about it. My body was sore a lot, but everybody was telling me I'd get used to it."

Just when Kevin got used to NBA practices, it was time to play in NBA games. Again, he was amazed at how physical they could be. After just a few minutes he found himself huffing and puffing. Although the Timberwolves needed new blood in the line-up, Coach Bill Blair refused to rush Kevin. He used him to spell members of the team's front line, including Christian Laettner, Sam Mitchell, and Tom Gugliotta. Kevin gave the team a nice boost of energy when he played. He usually scored a few baskets and grabbed a few rebounds, then sat down and watched the end of the game.

Kevin was not unhappy with his role—he understood that Blair and McHale were just getting him used to the league. But he was disappointed with his statistics. Kevin was used to seeing 25 points and 15 rebounds next to his name in the morning paper. This was embarrassing. The longer he sat, the more frustrated he became. The electric smile he flashed so often in the first few weeks was now nowhere to be found. Kevin

received word that McHale wanted to see him in his office. *Uh-oh*, he thought, *I'm in trouble.*

McHale told Kevin he was not in trouble. The team was concerned because they sensed he was discouraged. In order to learn and grow in the NBA, McHale explained, you have to be relaxed and be patient with yourself. Coach Blair, he said, had big plans for the second half of the season. But Kevin would not be a part of those plans if he did not stop worrying.

From that day on, Kevin was sensational. Whether he

Bill Blair gives an on-the-job lecture during Kevin's first NBA game.

> "The fact that he's willing to learn has really helped him."
>
> **KAREEM ABDUL-JABBAR**

played 5 minutes or 25 minutes, he did his best and learned from both his successes and his mistakes. At mid-season, the Timberwolves traded Laettner and gave his starting spot to Kevin. He scored in double figures and became the team's second-best rebounder. Kevin finished the year as Minnesota's most accurate shooter—an unheard-of feat for a rookie.

Kevin had a great season "off the court," too. He handled himself like a veteran on the road, and made the right kind of headlines at home in Minneapolis. Earlier in the season, when Laettner criticized Kevin in the press, he handled this tricky situation perfectly. He understood that the veteran Laettner was threatened by his presence, and that the team was looking to trade him. Rather than starting a war of words in the newspapers, he approached Laettner privately and they worked out their differences. Kevin then went to the Timberwolves and told them not to sweat it—the incident was taken care of. At twenty years old, he was not only ready to play in the NBA, but he was poised to become the team's leader.

Leader of the Pack

chapter 6

*"He has so much talent
that it will be almost scary
to see him this season."*

— ALL-STAR SCOTTIE PIPPEN

The Timberwolves finished the 1995–1996 season with just 26 victories. For the first time, however, they felt good about their future. Kevin was thinking about the team's future, too. He and Stephon Marbury, who was in school at Georgia Tech, had continued their phone friendship during the season. He knew that Marbury was planning to leave college and turn pro. Kevin began urging the team to draft Marbury even before he announced his decision. By draft day, McHale was convinced Minnesota should get him.

There were three great guards in the 1996 draft: Allen Iverson, Ray Allen, and Stephon Marbury. There were four teams picking ahead of the Timberwolves. The Philadelphia 76ers selected Iverson with the first overall pick. The next two teams took front-court players. The Milwaukee Bucks, picking fourth, grabbed Marbury. Thinking

Kevin's confidence soared in his second NBA season. Here he finishes a reverse slam against Kevin Willis, one of the league's toughest defenders.

quickly, McHale selected Ray Allen, then engineered a trade with the Bucks. He packaged Allen and a future draft pick, and Minnesota got Marbury after all.

The 1996–1997 Timberwolves had a new coach, Flip Saunders, sharp new uniforms, and a new winning attitude. One losing season was enough for Kevin, and he let everyone know it. In training camp, he chewed out veteran Stojko Vrankovic when he banked in a layup instead of dunking. After practice, he let the 32-year-old center know it was nothing personal, once again showing his knack for leadership.

Through the first half of the year, Kevin was very good. Despite a sprained ankle, he averaged 15 points, 9 rebounds, 3 assists, and 3 blocks per game. He was selected to participate in the NBA All-Star Game, making him the youngest player since his hero, Magic Johnson, to earn that honor. In the second half of the year, the Timberwolves made opponents howl. Kevin and Stephon were one of the best inside-outside duos in the league, and street-slick Tom Gugliotta fit right into things. By March, Minnesota had already surpassed its victory total from the previous season. By April, the Timberwolves were in the playoffs for the first time in franchise history. Kevin finished especially strong, boosting his scoring average up to 17 points per game.

As the playoffs neared and the Timberwolves looked back with pride on their first 40-win campaign, Kevin warned his teammates that they had to stay hungry. Things were going to get harder, not easier, once the playoffs began. "We can't let a little bit of success satisfy us," he said.

Unfortunately, his words seemed to fall on deaf ears. The Houston Rockets, a veteran team with championship experience, swept Minnesota out of the postseason. When the final buzzer sounded, superstar Charles Barkley went to Kevin and told him to keep his head up. He had played well, and his team should be proud. Barkley's gesture meant a lot to Kevin. Instead of starting the summer on a disappointing note, he was already getting psyched for his third NBA season.

The Garnett File

KEVIN'S FAVORITE...

Foods . . . . Hamburgers, Fries, and Pizza
Male Athlete . . . . Magic Johnson
Female Athlete . . . . . . Marion Jones
Books . . . . Beverly Cleary's "Ramona" series

"It's all about having fun. Play hard and fair, don't hurt anybody. Feel good about what you're doing and how you're doing it."

chapter 7

The Kid Who Changed
Everything

"The magnitude of Garnett's contract indicated the whole thing was out of control."

— NBA DEPUTY COMMISSIONER RUSS GRANIK

According to NBA rules, Kevin was allowed to request a contract extension after his second season. The Timberwolves suspected he would do this, so they sat down and discussed what the young man had already accomplished, and what they expected him to do in the years to come. Owner Glen Taylor listened to everyone's opinions and decided that Kevin should be signed to a long-term contract, regardless of the cost. With great fanfare, the team announced that it would bestow upon

> ## Did You Know?
> Although Kevin is listed at 6 feet 11 inches (211 cm), he says he has been measured at an even 7 feet (213 cm).

Kevin a record-smashing six-year $102 million contract. The Timberwolves wanted to show Kevin how much they appreciated him, and this seemed like a great way to do it.

What can I say? A day after signing the richest contract in league history, Kevin talks with the media.

To their amazement—and to the shock of almost everyone in sports—Eric Fleisher advised Kevin to turn down the deal.

The Timberwolves went back to the drawing board to figure their next move. They estimated that Kevin could make around $20 million a year if he were to sign with a team in a major media center like New York or Los Angeles, where he would have better opportunities to do commercials and movies. Unwilling to lose him, Taylor offered $21 million a season for a total of $126 million. It was more than he had paid for the entire team two years earlier!

This time Kevin said yes. Minnesota fans were ecstatic. Everyone else just shook their heads. What had sports come to, they wondered, when a player is worth more than the team he plays for? Taylor defended the offer by explaining what would have happened had he *not* paid Kevin. Fans would have stopped coming to the Target Center,

"It's hard to imagine anyone having his knowledge of the game at his age. Offensively, he has that wonderful turnaround jump shot and those follow-ups around the basket. He's one of those guys who, because of his size and athletic ability, creates real difficult defensive matchups."

JERRY WEST

and pro basketball in Minnesota would be destroyed. Keeping Kevin in town was the only way he knew of telling the fans the NBA was here to stay.

As the 1997–1998 season began, Taylor's investment looked like a smart one. To become a championship contender, a team has to have three "go-to" players; Gugliotta, Marbury, and Garnett made up the best young threesome in the league. Night in, night out, they combined for 50 to 60 points. During one stretch in January, the team won seven games in a row. By the All-Star break, the Timberwolves were one of the best clubs in the NBA's Western Conference, and Kevin was voted onto the All-Star team as a starter. When the reserves were named and Marbury and Gugliotta did not make it, fans of the Timberwolves howled their disappointment.

The second half of the season turned sour when Gugliotta was lost to a knee injury. With the Timberwolves already weak at center and lacking a consistent shooting guard, the team struggled just to make the playoffs. Still, Kevin finished with big numbers, and Minnesota ended up with a 45–37 record—by far the best in team history.

This did not take the sting out of yet another first-round loss. After leading the Timberwolves to two wins in three games against the Seattle Supersonics, Kevin watched in dismay as Gary Payton took charge of the series and single-handedly blew Minnesota out of the playoffs.

That spring, Kevin began to hear rumors that league owners wanted to renegotiate their basic agreement with the players. He also heard that the reason for this was the huge contract he had signed. Kevin had done nothing wrong—in fact, it was an agreement the owners had pushed through several years earlier that had enabled him to renegotiate his deal. But now they were having second thoughts and wanted to tip the scales back in their favor. When the NBA Players Union heard the league's proposal, it refused to accept it. The owners retaliated by "locking out" the players on July 1.

The dispute continued for months, with neither side willing to budge. When the lockout dragged into November, the league started canceling games. The NBA claimed it was willing to cancel the entire season if the players did not give in. During the negotiations, Kevin's name came up again and again. He felt bad that he was the "cause" of the dispute, but after all the owners had mismanaged their finances, hadn't they? Eventually, the players bowed to the league's demands, and the season was saved.

Talk To Me, KG

Kevin is regarded as one of the NBA's best interviews. Quotes like these show why:

"I leave my heart on the court every night. I earn my keep."

"I want to stand out. After my career is over, I want people to say, 'He was different.' It's not to be outrageous. I just want people to know that when I played ball, I was having fun."

"Satisfied? No, I'm not satisfied. There's a lot I want to get done in the NBA and that ain't happening yet."

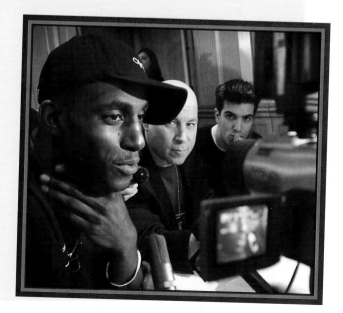

Dream Teamer

chapter 8

"*I've never seen anyone who wants to win as badly as he does.*"
— SUPERSTAR TIM DUNCAN

By the time play resumed in the 1998–1999 season, there were just 50 games left. There were some new faces on the team, including Joe Smith and—of all people, Kevin's role model—Malik Sealy! Gone was Tom Gugliotta, who signed with the Phoenix Suns as a free agent. Six weeks into the season, the team traded Stephon Marbury to New Jersey. He claimed he did not like Minnesota and wanted to play closer to home. In a three-way deal, the Timberwolves acquired point guard Terrell Brandon and draft picks. With so many new players and so little time to get used to one another, the Timberwolves were out of sync for much of the season.

Everyone, that is, except Kevin. His numbers improved for the fourth year in a row, as he averaged more than 20 points and 10 rebounds a night. Were it not for his con-

Malik Sealy scores over Tim Duncan. Kevin was thrilled when his boyhood idol joined the team, but Sealy could not keep the Spurs from defeating Minnesota in the playoffs.

sistency and leadership, the Timberwolves would have missed the playoffs. As it was, they barely made it. This time they ran into San Antonio's Twin Towers, David Robinson and Tim Duncan. Kevin did his best King Kong imitation and tried to handle both players at once, but he was fighting a losing battle. The Spurs won the series in four games.

From the disappointment of the "lockout season" came the excitement of joining Team USA. The United States sent Kevin and 11 other players to Puerto Rico for the three-game Olympic qualifying tournament. Kevin had watched the original Dream Team play in Barcelona, Spain, during the 1992 Summer Games and could hardly believe he was wearing the same uniform that Michael Jordan and Magic

As he has gotten bigger, stronger, and more experienced, Kevin's power moves have made him one of the NBA's best.

Johnson once did. Even though the Americans won as expected in Puerto Rico, it was still an honor. "There are thousands of players who could have been selected for the team," Kevin says. "To be one of the twelve chosen means a lot, not only about your talent, but also about your character. They are not just going to send anyone over there who has a bad attitude or bad character, so when you get chosen, people are telling you that you've got skills and you're a good guy."

While several players just went through the motions during the competition, Kevin's enthusiasm shone through. The others teased him about being so excited, but when Team USA took the court the Puerto Rican fans cheered his hustle and spirited play while booing some of the other NBA superstars. Behind the scenes, Kevin assumed a leadership role, especially with the two college players invited to join the team. He got angry at Richard Hamilton for missing a team breakfast, and scolded Wally Szczerbiak for not boxing

This is how opponents would like to see Kevin "in the paint." On the basketball court, he is impossible to stop when he gets position down low.

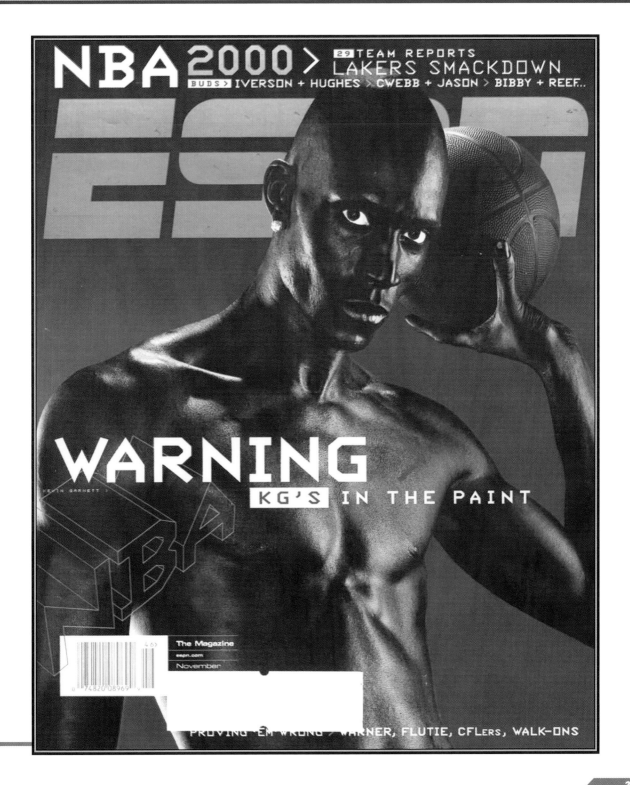

NBA 2000 > 29 TEAM REPORTS
LAKERS SMACKDOWN
BUDS > IVERSON + HUGHES > CWEBB + JASON > BIBBY + REEF...

WARNING
KG'S IN THE PAINT

The Magazine
espn.com
November

0 74820 08969 4 6>

PROVING 'EM WRONG > WARNER, FLUTIE, CFLers, WALK-ONS

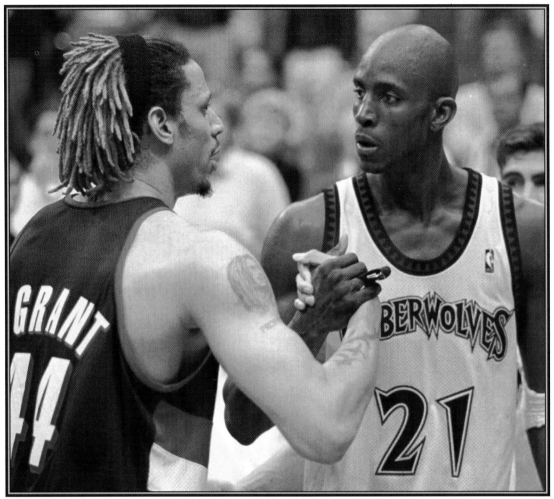

Kevin congratulates Brian Grant after the Trail Blazers knocked Minnesota out of the 2000 playoffs. Kevin is a good sport, but he hates losing.

out on a rebound during practice. Kevin was extra-loud with Szczerbiak, probably because the Timberwolves had just drafted him.

Kevin returned for the 1999–2000 season ready for a big year. The Timberwolves had a nice blend of young talent and veteran experience. So when the team got off to a sluggish start, Coach Saunders had a lot of options. The one he chose was Malik Sealy, the team's reserve shooting guard. Saunders benched Anthony Peeler in December and inserted Sealy into the starting lineup. The former St. John's star energized Minnesota with his tenacious defense, and he hit a lot of big shots. The Timberwolves began rolling. Kevin was named NBA Player of the Week over Christmas, then went out and celebrated with a club-record 23 rebounds against the Orlando Magic.

One of the highlights of this season for Kevin was becoming close friends with Sealy. Kevin shyly admitted that he had once chosen him as a role model. Sealy was flattered. It never occurred to him that he was the reason why Kevin wore number 21. With the two friends providing leadership, the Timberwolves cruised to a remarkable 50-win season. The fans chose Kevin as an All-Star starter, and he earned First-Team All-NBA and All-Defense honors for the first time. He also was named NBA Player of the Week a total of three times.

This time the Timberwolves faced the Portland Trail Blazers in the first round of the playoffs. Portland's balanced attack—which featured stars like Scottie Pippen, Damon Stoudamire, Steve Smith, Rasheed Wallace, and Arvidas Sabonis—was just too much for Minnesota, which fell in four hard-fought games. Once again, Kevin was left to ponder the meaning of another early postseason exit.

Did You Know?

It turned out that playing in a small market like Minneapolis did not hurt Kevin's endorsement opportunities. When you are as good as he is, you could probably play on a desert island and get noticed! Indeed, in his short career, Kevin has done ads for everything from American Express to "Got Milk?"

"The best defenders have focus. So you have to focus on your man and on what your responsibility is."

KEVIN GARNETT, DEFENDING AGAINST DAVID ROBINSON

Funeral for a Friend

chapter 9

> *"I'm still not over it. I can't even really talk about it."*
>
> — **KEVIN GARNETT**

Malik Sealy

Since Kevin's days as a kid in Nickeltown, basketball had always filled some void in his life. On May 20, 2000, he experienced an emptiness that a million jump shots could not fill. That was the day he learned that Malik Sealy had died. He was driving home at night when a drunk swerved into his lane and hit him head-on. Sealy had no chance to react; he was killed instantly. Kevin had been sad before, but he had never felt this bad.

When it was time to leave for the Olympics, Kevin welcomed the chance to get away. Team USA stopped in Hawaii to practice for a few days, then proceeded to Australia. Kevin had a great time. He visited a wildlife park, made friends with athletes

Kevin (top left) is still in shock as he serves as one of the pallbearers at Malik Sealy's funeral.

Kevin and high-school rival Vince Carter share a golden moment in Sydney after Team USA won the Olympic basketball tournament.

from other nations, and walked proudly into the stadium during the opening ceremonies in Sydney.

Once the basketball began, Kevin's hustle made him a crowd favorite, just as it had in Puerto Rico. This time, however, Team USA really needed his energy. Lithuania, which gave Kevin and his teammates a tough time in the opening round, nearly won in the semifinals. The U.S. was lucky to escape with an 85–83 win. In the gold-medal game against France, Team USA also struggled before pulling out a 10-point victory in the second half. Kevin wondered whether the Americans were that bad, or whether

Kevin honored Malik Sealy with a special tattoo, as well as wearing his name and numbers on his elbow pads.

the rest of the world was getting that good. Either way, he had his gold medal.

Back in Minnesota, Kevin prepared for his biggest season. He was coming into his own as a player—there was little he could not do on the basketball court. Now he wanted to lift the Timberwolves into the playoffs and past the first round. To honor his fallen friend, Kevin had a special tattoo created in Malik Sealy's memory. He also requested that the team keep a locker empty both at home and on the road.

Kevin was a whirlwind. He dominated at both ends, and established himself as the NBA's most dynamic young leader. Kevin averaged 22 points and 5 assists per game, and also blossomed into the NBA's best all-around defender. During the year he guarded centers, power forwards, and small forwards, and shut everyone down. His mark of 11.4 rebounds per game was sixth best in basketball.

For the first time since Kevin's arrival in Minnesota, the Timberwolves seemed to have a team that could get deep into the playoffs. Wally Szczerbiak was a quick learner, Terrell Brandon could do it all at point guard, and Anthony Peeler had become one of the NBA's better long-range shooters.

The team had its ups and downs during the year, but finished with a respectable 47 victories. However, for some reason the Timberwolves were not ready to compete in

Kevin tried to be a one-man show in 2001, but he could not carry the team past the first round of the playoffs.

the postseason. In the final weeks, Szczerbiak had stopped working hard to get open, Brandon had stopped penetrating, Peeler had become inconsistent from three-point range, and whomever Coach Saunders sent in to play center was simply not getting the job done. Kevin was better than ever, but his teammates sometimes just "stood around" and watched him.

Minnesota's first-round opponent—once again the San Antonio Spurs—saw this and took advantage of it. Although the Timberwolves made the series interesting, they exited the playoffs for the fifth year in a row after only one round. "With every bad thing, you try to find something good and take that away," says Kevin of his team's failure to advance in the postseason. "But you know, I don't want to hear that anymore. I want to get to the big dance."

KID *STUFF*

What are other NBA stars saying about Da Kid?

"He's into the game and ready to play."
TIM HARDAWAY

"He's a fiery young player that likes to win . . . he likes to get the job done."
VINCE CARTER (TOP RIGHT)

"He improves his game each year, and that's why he's one of the top players in the world."
JASON KIDD

"KG is probably double the person that he is the basketball player."
VIN BAKER

"He's probably one of the most unique players in the world."
ALLAN HOUSTON (BOTTOM RIGHT)

"He makes everybody better."
SHAREEF ABDUR-RAHIM

Staying and Playing

chapter 10

> *"I'm nowhere near where
> I want to be as a player."*
> — **KEVIN GARNETT**

During one of the Timberwolves' slumps in the 2000–2001 season, some fans began wondering whether the team might be better off trading Kevin and rebuilding. Local newspapers and radio stations began picking up on this idea, and soon it became the city's hottest issue. By dealing Kevin to another club, the Timberwolves could get two good players, and have enough "room" under the league's salary cap to sign one or two more. Was it worth letting a great player go to get a few good

Did You Know?

Kevin is taking college courses on the Internet from the University of Missouri.

ones? Kevin did not think so. Besides, it was hard for him to imagine playing for anyone else. The Timberwolves were the only team he had ever known, and the team he wanted to take to the "big dance."

Kevin is a picture of concentration as he goes up for two points in the NBA All-Star Game.

In Kevin's mind, contending for a championship is a simple matter of finding the right mix of players who are willing to do whatever it takes to win. As he likes to say, "If you do all the little things well, it will add up to big things."

Kevin's sentiments were echoed by thousands of fans. They called, wrote, and e-mailed their positive feelings about KG. It made him proud to know the people of Minnesota were behind him. Still, after six NBA seasons and five straight playoff disappointments, Kevin is getting impatient for the success he has found elsewhere in his basketball life. Yet, he is hardly discouraged. If anything, he just wants it more. As for his goals, Kevin would like to win a Most Valuable Player trophy and, above all else, an NBA championship.

Of course, he knows that those accomplishments take good luck and perfect timing—things that are not always under his control. So Kevin tends to think about the bigger picture when he talks about how he would like to be remembered. "I would love to do something that would make everybody I care about proud that Kevin Garnett was around," he says.

pro *stats*

Season	Team	Games	Shooting Pct.	Assists/ Game	Rebounds/ Game	Blocks/ Game	Points/ Game
1995–96	Timberwolves	80	49.1	1.8	6.3	1.6	10.4
1996–97	Timberwolves	77	49.9	3.1	8.0	2.1	17.0
1997–98	Timberwolves	82	49.1	4.2	9.6	1.8	18.5
1998–99	Timberwolves	47	46.0	4.3	10.4	1.8	20.8
1999–00	Timberwolves	81	49.7	5.0	11.8	1.6	22.9
2000–01	Timberwolves	81	47.7	5.0	11.4	1.8	22.0
Totals		**448**	**48.7**	**3.9**	**9.5**	**1.8**	**18.5**

pro *achievements*

First-Team All-NBA 2001

First-Team All-Defense 2001

Member of Olympic "Dream Team" 2000

First All-Star Starter in Timberwolves History 1998

NBA All-Star 1997, 1998, 2000, 2001

Kevin has been asked a lot of questions in his short life—some very good ones, and some very bad ones—and he has become quite good at answering all of them. In fact, he was honored by NBA writers as a member of their "all-interview" team! That is one reason he finds it kind of funny that the question he is finally comfortable answering is the one almost no one asks him anymore: *Does he regret skipping college and going straight to the pros?* "I'm happy I made the decision that I did," Kevin says. "I'm not looking back, only forward."

Does he feel he missed out on something? "Probably," he admits. "But what I may have missed doesn't come close to comparing with what I've gained."

As Kevin enters his prime years, he hopes to accomplish even more, both on and off the court. There sometimes seems to be no limit to what he can do, especially when he gets that look in his eye and Da Kid comes out. Which raises another question: How long can people keep calling him that?

According to Kevin, there is no need to stop. "I'll always have a kid in me," he says.

The kid in Kevin comes out in every game.
It has made him one of the most popular players in the NBA.

Index